MW01595578

AMERICAN GIRL BOOK ABOUT PUBERTY

A GUIDE TO CARE AND KEEPING OF YOUR BODY

Dr. C. Albert

Copyright©2021 Dr. C. Albert

All Rights Reserved

TABLE OF CONTENT

HELP FOR BREAST HURT
WHEN TO SEE A SPECIALIST

PARENT FAQS ABOUT GIRLS AND THEIR EVOLVING BODIES:

INTRODUCTION

Puberty can be an energizing however troublesome time for some children. During Puberty, your body changes into that of a grown-up. These progressions can happen gradually or rapidly. It's typical for certain individuals to go through Puberty sooner than others.

Puberty for the most part begins anyplace between the ages of 9 and 15 in young men and 8 and 13 in young ladies. The wide scope of time during which Puberty ordinarily hits is the reason a portion of your companions may look more seasoned than others.

Puberty is important for the common developing cycle. During puberty, your body will become quicker than at some other time in your life, aside from when you were a child. Puberty will not start until chemicals delivered by the pituitary organ in your mind tell your body that now is the ideal time.

You may once in a while wish that you could begin Puberty quicker. Sadly, there's very little you can do to control the circumstance of Puberty. In any case, in the event that you haven't begun Puberty at this point, you have additional time left to develop.

5

When every one of the indications of Puberty is there, you're generally near your grown-up tallness.

It assists with recalling that basically everybody goes through Puberty in the long run. It's entirely typical to feel confounded or disappointed.

When does Puberty begin in young ladies?

In young ladies, Puberty for the most part starts at some point between the ages of 8 and 13. Puberty in young ladies starts when the pituitary organ advises the ovaries that it's an ideal opportunity to begin creating a chemical called estrogen. Estrogen changes your body during Puberty and makes you equipped for getting pregnant.

The first indication of Puberty in quite a while is generally developing Breasts. You may see that your Breasts are expanding or taking on an alternate shape. Most young ladies don't get their periods until around two years after the Breasts start to develop.

Different indications of Puberty in Girls include:

• getting taller rapidly

• changing body shape (more extensive hips, bends)

• wider hips

• weight acquire

• hair in the armpits and crotch

• acne

On the off chance that your Breasts haven't started creating by age 13, specialists would consider your Puberty postponed. Most young ladies with deferred Puberty acquire this condition from their folks. They normally find their companions inside a couple of years.

A low level of muscle to fat ratio can defer Puberty in certain young ladies. This is basic in young ladies who are athletic. Different reasons for deferred Puberty incorporate hormonal issues and a background marked by clinical issues, similar to a malignancy.

What to do in the event that you haven't hit Puberty yet

Puberty will occur when your body is prepared for it. However, sitting tight for Puberty can be hard. You may feel humiliated, on edge, and discouraged about postponed Puberty. Here are a couple of things that may help:

• **Speak up**. In case you're stressed over your turn of events, don't remain quiet about it. Offer your concerns to your folks or companions. Discussing this stuff will cause you to feel less alone.

• **Get an exam**. Your PCP has seen huge loads of children go through Puberty. During an actual test, your PCP can keep an eye on the advancement of your body and advise you if everything is ordinary. In the event that fundamental, your primary care physician can likewise perform tests to check your chemical levels.

• **Ask your primary care physician about treatment.** On the off chance that your PCP makes a determination of deferred Puberty, they may suggest treatment. Your primary care physician can give you a medicine for chemical drugs that will trigger the beginning of Puberty.

- **Educate yourself**. The more you think about Puberty, the more agreeable you will feel with your body. Finding out about Puberty can likewise make it simpler to discuss.

- **Connect with different children like you**. Since your companions aren't discussing postponed Puberty doesn't mean you're distant from everyone else. Talk with a parent or confided in a grown-up. They can help you discover online networks of children managing deferred Puberty. You may be astonished how acceptable it feels to trade stories.

- **Eat good food**. A solid eating regimen is vital for your developing body. Eating an eating routine loaded with natural products, vegetables, and sound proteins will give your body the fuel it needs to develop.

- **Get dynamic**. A functioning way of life is additionally critical to your general wellbeing. Consider joining a games group or going for a run with your parent.

•   **Don't try too hard**. While both smart dieting and actual work are significant for your general wellbeing, inordinate slimming down or exercise can add to deferred Puberty. Converse with your folks and specialist on the off chance that you have inquiries concerning the amount to eat or work out.

•   **Be patient**. It very well may be hard to appear to be unique from your companions, yet most children will get up to speed normally. When your Puberty, at last, shows up, you'll form into a solid grown-up.

Signs Your Period is Coming

First Period Side effects?

Find out how to peruse and comprehend these signs! Here are 3 useful hints to prepare for this exceptional time!

Although some young girls get their first period somewhere in the range of 11 and 13 years of age, you could go anyplace somewhere in the range of 9 and 16. Everybody has her own "organic clock," and yours is not quite the same as anybody else's. So regardless of whether you sense that you'll never get your period, don't stress, you will! How do you realize it's as it would prefer? Watch for these signs.

First Period Manifestations. Puberty in itself is a major sign that your first period's on its way. Here is a couple to pay special mind to, as well:

1.   **Developing Breast "buds"**: It can take three to four years for your Breasts to then completely grow, however, you can expect your period around two years after your Breasts begin creating.

2.   **Growing pubic hair**: Soon after your Breasts begin to shape, you'll most likely beginning developing pubic hair. It will be delicate and dainty from the start, however, it'll get coarser over the long run. Your period normally shows up around one to two years after.

3.   **Discharge**: Vaginal release (white or yellowish liquid) is normally a definite sign that your first period is on its way. You might need to begin utilizing Consistently pantiliners to secure your clothing. Your period should begin in the following, not many months! You will discover

more data about the vaginal release in our article Vaginal release: Disgusting yet Astonishing.

Notwithstanding this body transformation, you can likewise ask your mother when she began her period. All things considered, you'll get your first period inside a year or so of when she got hers. In addition, it's a happy chance to have a discussion with your mother about pretty much every one of the progressions you're encountering. She can likewise help you track down the correct items.

Getting ready for Your First Period

Since no one can really tell when your first period will show up, it's an extraordinary thought to be prepared. Here are a few thoughts:

• Prepare a survival pack containing a pantiliner, cushion, and clean clothing in a tactful sack

• Keep a pantiliner or cushion in your book pack or handbag

• In a crisis, tissue can work until you can get a pantiliner or cushion

• Ask a companion, school medical attendant, or educator for help — most schools save additional pantiliners or cushions for precisely this explanation!

The Phases of Puberty in Girls

As a grown-up, you presumably recall Puberty cause when your body went through a lot of changes. What's more, presently you're the parent of a youngster who's encountering these changes. You'll need to realize what's in store so you can help your kid through each phase of improvement. find out about the Leather expert stages and what you can hope to find in young ladies during each stage.

Leather expert stage 1

Leather expert stage 1 portrays a youngster's appearance before any actual indications of Puberty show up. At the finish of stage 1, the mind is simply beginning to convey messages to the body to plan for changes.

The nerve center starts to deliver gonadotropin-delivering chemicals and goes to the pituitary organ, which is the little region under the cerebrum that makes chemicals that control different organs in the body.

The pituitary organ additionally makes two different chemicals: luteinizing chemical and follicle animating chemical.

These early signals ordinarily start after a young lady's eighth birthday celebration and after a kid's ninth or tenth birthday celebration. There aren't any perceptible actual changes for young men or young ladies at this stage.

Leather expert stage 2

Stage 2 denotes the start of the actual turn of events. Chemicals start to convey messages all through the body.

Puberty typically begins between ages 9 and 11. The main indications of Breasts called "buds," begin to frame under the areola. They might be irritated or delicate, which is ordinary.

It's regular for Breasts to be of various sizes and develop at various rates. Along these lines, it's ordinary on the off chance that one bud seems bigger than the other. The hazier territory around the (areola) will likewise grow.

Moreover, the uterus starts to get bigger, and modest quantities of pubic hair begin developing on the lips of the vagina.

All things considered, Individuals of color start Puberty a year prior to white young ladies, and are ahead with regards to Breast improvement and having their first periods. Likewise, young ladies with a higher weight list experience a prior beginning of Puberty.

Leather expert stage 3

Actual changes are getting more self-evident.

Actual changes in young ladies generally start after age 12. These progressions include:

• Breast "buds" proceed to develop and extend.

• Pubic hair gets thicker and curlier.

• Hair begins framing under the armpits.

• The first indications of skin inflammation may show up on the face and back.

• The most noteworthy development rate for tallness starts (around 3.2 inches each year).

- Hips and thighs begin to develop fat.

Attempt the first-class application for contemplation and rest

Experience 100+ guided reflections with Quiet's honor-winning contemplation application. Intended for all experience levels, and accessible when you need it most in your day. Start your free preliminary today.

Leather expert stage 4

Puberty is going all out during stage 4. The two young men and young ladies are seeing numerous changes.

In young ladies, stage 4 for the most part begins around age 13. Changes include:

- Breasts take on a more full shape, passing the bud stage.

- Many young ladies get their first period, regularly between ages of 12 and 14, however, it can happen prior.

- Height development will back off to around 2 to 3 inches each year.

- Pubic hair gets thicker.

Leather treater stage 5

This last stage denotes the finish of your kid's actual development.

In young ladies, stage 5 normally occurs around age 15. Changes include:

- Breasts arrive at rough grown-up size and shape, however, Breasts can keep on changing through age 18.

- Periods become customary following a half year to two years.

- Girls arrive at grown-up tallness one to two years after their first period.

- Pubic hair rounds out to arrive at the internal thighs.

- Reproductive organs and privates are completely evolved.

•   Hips, thighs, and bottom round outfit as a fiddle.

SKIN INFLAMMATION

Skin inflammation can be an issue for young ladies. The changing chemicals cause oils to develop on the skin and stop up pores. Your youngster can create skin inflammation on the face, back, or chest.

A few groups have more awful skin inflammation than others. On the off chance that you have a family background of skin inflammation, there's a higher chance your kid will likewise encounter skin inflammation.

By and large, you can treat skin break out by washing the influenced zones consistently with a gentle cleanser. What's more, there are additionally ludicrous creams and balms to help control breakouts. You might need to attempt some home cures also.

For more serious skin inflammation, you may think about taking your youngster to see their pediatrician or a dermatologist. The specialist can suggest more grounded remedy medicines.

Personal stench

Bigger perspiration organs likewise create during Puberty. To forestall stench, converse with your kid about antiperspirant choices and ensure they shower routinely, particularly after extraordinary actual work. Get familiar with cleanliness propensities for youngsters and teenagers.

Showing support

Puberty can be trying for youngsters and guardians. As well as causing numerous actual changes, chemicals are additionally causing passionate changes. You may see your youngster is irritable or carrying on in an unexpected way.

It's imperative to respond with tolerance and comprehension. Your youngster might be feeling uncertain about their evolving body, including their skin break out.

Discussion about these progressions and console your youngster it's an ordinary piece of development. In the event that something is especially alarming, converse with your youngster's PCP too.

Breast Improvement

It is typical for young ladies and teens to have bunches of inquiries regarding their Breasts as they begin to create.

Seeing the body change can be overwhelming, and it is completely typical to stress over what's in store.

Here are some normal inquiries and answers about Breast improvement to help manage youngsters through the cycle.

Should Breasts hurt when they develop?

Numerous young ladies experience torment as their Breasts develop and this isn't anything to stress over.

Breasts create as the chemicals estrogen and progesterone are delivered at Puberty.

These chemicals make the Breast tissue develop. As it does, the encompassing skin may extend, which is one explanation Breasts can hurt when they develop.

The chemicals that invigorate Breast development are another explanation they may hurt. Chemicals change the degrees of liquid in the Breast tissue, which can make the Breasts more touchy and surprisingly hurt.

In the event that a young lady has begun her period, her Breasts may likewise hurt around her feminine cycle. These throbs are because of hormonal changes and are an ordinary piece of the period.

For what reason do red imprints show up on Breasts?

As Breast tissue develops, the encompassing skin needs to stretch to oblige the expanding size.

At times the skin doesn't extend adequately quick and the center layer tears marginally, making red stretch imprints show up. This happens to many, if not most, youngsters and ought not to be a reason for shame.

There are heaps of creams accessible in the drug store to help lessen the presence of these imprints. Over the long haul, the lines blur to white all alone and are not particularly observable.

Is it typical for Breasts to be of various sizes?

It is totally typical for every one of a lady's two Breasts to develop at various rates. In any event, when completely created, they might be of various sizes. Having Breasts of inconsistent size is seldom a wellbeing concern, regardless of whether they are an entire cup size unique.

Unevenly estimated Breasts are not typically something that any other person would see, yet young ladies can once in a while act naturally aware of this distinction. Utilizing cushioning on one side of a bra can help young ladies feel more sure.

Could a Breast lump mean there is malignancy?

A Breast knot found while Breasts are developing might be innocuous. Notwithstanding, a specialist ought to be counseled if there are concerns.

At the point when Breasts start to develop, they show up as a bump under the areola. This is an ordinary piece of the improvement cycle.

Most knots are fibroadenomas or an excess of connective tissue in the Breast. High school irregularities are dangerous in not many cases.

While all things considered, a Breast irregularity that is found while Breasts are developing is innocuous, ladies of any age are encouraged to be comfortable with their Breasts. This will permit them to detect any progressions that happen.

At the point when Breasts are completely evolved, ladies should self-look at them consistently. In the event that they discover protuberances that are not ordinarily there once their Breasts have quit developing, it is a smart thought to address a specialist. Normally, the specialist can rapidly preclude malignancy.

Could young fellows create Breast tissue?

While it doesn't occur to everybody, it isn't strange for young fellows to build up some Breast tissue on their chests as they go through Puberty.

This is called gynecomastia. It is because of hormonal changes, and any Breast tissue that develops is ordinarily transitory.

Notwithstanding not being phenomenal, gynecomastia can be disturbing for young fellows on the off chance that they don't comprehend why it is going on. On the off chance that a young fellow is worried about this, they ought to address their primary care physician for guidance.

Indications of Breast advancement

At the point when a young lady begins to create Breasts, she may recognize the accompanying signs:

•   firm protuberances, called Breast buds, felt under the areola

•   the chest feeling delicate around every areola

•   itchiness around the areolas and chest territory

Stages

There are five phases of Breast improvement. These stages start from birth and progress as a young lady goes through Puberty.

1.   The tip of the areola is raised from birth, however, the remainder of the chest is level.

2.   Breast buds structure as firm protuberances under every areola, raised from the chest. As this occurs, the space of hazier skin around the areola called the areola may get greater.

3.   The Breasts get marginally bigger as Breast tissue creates.

4.   The areola and areola raise up, shaping a second hill over the Breast tissue.

5.   The Breast gets adjusted with just the areola raised. This is the last phase of improvement.

Breasts may proceed to change and create over an individual's lifetime. Hormonal cycles, pregnancy, Breast taking care of, and menopause all influence the Breasts.

BREAST CARE

Offer on Pinterest Once the Breasts have created, picking an effectively fitted bra is suggested.

When a young lady has built up her Breasts, it is significant that she cares for them, likewise with some other piece of her body.

Ensuring bras or tops fit well, on the off chance that she chooses to wear them for help, is significant. It is likewise prescribed to have some time without wearing a bra, so the skin can relax.

Ladies additionally need to check their Breasts consistently for knots and other admonition indications of Breast malignancy. A specialist can clarify the cycle, or ladies can peruse guides on the web.

Help for Breast hurt

Breast torments and hurts regularly pass rapidly. In any case, on the off chance that they don't disappear all alone, there are medicines that can help. These incorporate over-the-counter painkillers, like ibuprofen, and agony calming gels.

Wearing a strong bra top or sports bra when practicing can likewise limit torment.

When to see a specialist

In the event that a youngster finds that torment, when their Breasts are developing, is hard to control, they ought to address a specialist. A specialist may recommend a drug to help control chemical levels if the torment is especially awful.

Seldom, a young lady may discover a knot in her breast that isn't clarified by the ordinary phases of Breast improvement. On the off chance that this occurs, it is in every case best to address a specialist to preclude any wellbeing concerns.

Parent FAQs about Girls and their evolving bodies:

I've heard that young ladies are getting their periods at more youthful and more youthful ages. Is this valid?

There is some discussion on this. The short response to this inquiry: possibly. Plainly the beginning age for Puberty has diminished in the course of the most recent 150 years, likely identified with improved nourishment. Patterns in Puberty in the course of the most recent 40 years are less clear. A few examinations recommend that Puberty is beginning prior in the US and Europe.

Prior Puberty can be found in kids who were conceived minuscule as babies (called little for gestational age), and we don't completely comprehend why this occurs. Corpulence is likewise a danger factor for prior Puberty, to a limited extent since muscle versus fat is engaged with how the body measures chemicals like estrogen.

By and large, more data and exploration is required on this subject so we can completely comprehend these examples and the potential purposes for them.

My little girl is stressed over putting on weight during Puberty. Is weight acquisition part of ordinary Puberty?

Indeed. As youth are becoming taller, it's not unexpected to put on weight. Rising measures of estrogen in the body additionally cause fat to store in the hips and Breasts, and the general level of muscle versus fat expansions in young ladies as they go through Puberty. Weight acquire that is beyond what expected during Puberty could be a reason for concern, however. Your pediatrician will search for whether your kid's weight acquires crosses percentile lines on her development graph or whether her weight list is more noteworthy than the 85th percentile. In any case, the general example of weight acquire is a higher priority than a specific number.

When considering the solid way of life and weight acquire, recall that propensities like active work and smart dieting grow very early—the same goes for the improvement of undesirable food inclinations and an excess of screen time. Ask your pediatrician for thoughts on the best way to fuse solid propensities into your family's ordinary schedules.

I need my 9-year-old girl to be ready for her first period, yet she's so youthful! When would it be a

good idea for me to begin conversing with her about periods?

By and large, most young ladies get their periods a normal of 2 – 2 ½ years after the advancement of Breast buds. The advancement of Breast buds is an extraordinary chance to speak more about body changes on the way. Accentuate that periods are typical, are important for having a solid body, and are not something to be embarrassed or humiliated about. Young ladies may feel uneasy about difficult periods or restless that their colleagues will discover. While each young lady is extraordinary, a consoling methodology and sufficient data can frequently soothe a portion of the uneasiness young ladies may feel about periods.

It's vastly improved for your girl to be educated about her body from the get-go during the time spent Puberty than to be astounded or even terrified as these progressions occur. It can likewise be useful to have sterile napkins accessible early and disclose how to utilize them before her first period shows up.

Talk transparently and really about Puberty. Answer any inquiries she may have about the progressions in her body. You might not need to know each answer, yet realize pediatricians are extraordinary assets for any inquiries regarding Puberty that you or your youngster have en route!

When should my girl have a pelvic test?

Sound young people needn't bother with a pelvic test until they are 21 years of age. Before yearly pelvic tests with pap, spreads were suggested for teens who were explicitly dynamic, yet research has shown that this isn't required. Pap spreads search for proof of human papilloma infection (HPV) disease, which can make pre-destructive and malignant changes to the cervix. We've found out increasingly more about HPV lately, including that young people are substantially more prone to clear the HPV contamination all alone, without the need for clinical intercession. Pap spreads before age 21 are just suggested for uncommon cases, like teenagers with HIV or invulnerable inadequacies. Pelvic tests are not done as a feature of routine medical care however might be essential in specific circumstances: for instance, if an explicitly dynamic juvenile has stomach torment.

When should young ladies be instructed on how to perform self-Breast tests? Will her pediatrician talk with her about this?

Young ladies by and large don't have to perform Breast self-tests since they are amazingly generally safe of Breast malignancy. Likewise, their Breasts are probably going to change as they develop, and the improvement of delicacy and expansion can be typical during changes in the feminine cycle. These ordinary changes can now and again prompt nervousness for young ladies who are performing standard Breast tests. The examination additionally has not shown a profit by Breast self-tests in the conclusion of Breast malignancy. Presently, we don't suggest routine Breast self-tests for pediatric patients, and there are varying rules for the proposals for grown-ups.

How would I regard my girl's requirement for security while likewise checking her turn of events?

Offer your little girl freedoms to discuss Puberty and the progressions that accompany it. Speaking transparently about Puberty can help forestall disgrace and shame, and may urge your girl to be more able to converse with you about the thing she is encountering. Nonetheless, a few children basically don't have any desire to converse with their folks about this sort of thing, and that is OK as well. Ensure your little girl realizes that you're free in the event that she has any inquiries and that she approaches confided in assets for data. These incorporate books and suitable wellbeing training at school. In the event that you have explicit worries about your youngster's turn of events or movement through Puberty, your pediatrician would be glad to address them with you and your girl.

Keep in mind: Discussing Puberty ought not simply to be a one-time conversation.

Data can be partaken in more modest discussions, opening the entryway for continuous correspondence with the goal that your girl can pose inquiries at her own speed. This open entryway will assist with discussions about other significant points as it were like sound connections, sex, sexuality, assent, and wellbeing (like how to forestall explicitly communicated disease and pregnancy, and substance use). Assemble a decent structure ahead of schedule for conversations later.

Made in the USA
Coppell, TX
12 August 2022

81320869R00020